KEYWORDS

words of **testimony** that open the **gates**
of every **stronghold** in your **metron**

STEVE PIXLER

CONTINUUM MINISTRY RESOURCES | MANSFIELD, TX

KEYWORDS | Words of Testimony That Open the Gates of Every Stronghold In Your Metron

STEVE PIXLER

Published by Continuum Ministry Resources, Mansfield, TX.
More resources available at stevepixler.com.

Keywords is a print book and eBook produced from the *Keywords* video series notes on YouTube. Check out the YouTube series on the Steve Pixler channel.

ISBN: 978-0-9914552-2-5

INTRODUCTION

Recently, I preached a message at our church—Freedom Life Church in Mansfield, TX—on *Keywords*. I preached out of a phrase I heard a while back while getting ready for bed one night:

"Words are keys."

I paused and processed. It came back stronger, "Words are keys." I had been working a bit through Matthew 16 and Jesus' statement about the "keys of the kingdom of heaven," so immediately my mind went there. And there, my friends, it stayed.

For days.

I just kept hearing, "Words are keys."

Of course, I had learned over many years about the power of our words. That should be Kingdom 101 for all of us. But this phrase was hooked up to something bigger that I knew God was a trying to tell me. This was not just "the power of positive speaking." This was God showing me something about *how* the kingdom of God comes in the world. In the real world.

Father God kept drawing my mind back to how kingdom believers are assigned a "metron" (an "area of influence") in family, business, church and everywhere else. And he kept saying to me, every believer has a metron; and every metron has strongholds; and every stronghold has gates; and every gate has keys...

Ah, there it is! "Words are keys."

Quite literally, Father was saying to me that the words we speak open up areas of kingdom influence by which the rule of Jesus breaks into the world.

That's what this little book with modest aspirations to grow up into more than a booklet is all about. How words we speak grow into *keywords*, words of testimony that open the gates of every stronghold in our metron.

Now, to make sense of all that we need to define the terms. And we shall presently. But for now, here is a summary statement, coiled up into one of the longest, run-on sentences found outside of the Epistles of Paul:

> God's strategy for saving the world is to multiply the Presence of Jesus by filling believers with the Spirit of Christ, the Holy Spirit; commission believers to serve in the world in an assigned metron—what Paul calls our "area of influence"; enact the dominion that Christ won at the cross over the gates of hell, which control passage (ingress/egress) to and from the strongholds that evil spirits, the strongmen, use to dominate and control human behavior on a personal, familial and societal level; and release

4

the shalom of heaven until "the knowledge of the glory of the Lord covers the earth as the waters cover the sea" and the blessing of Abraham transforms the nations.

Did you get that? If not, read it again. Or thrice.

Now. Let's get to the heavy lifting. Terms need defining, and there's no one but you and me to do it. So let's get to it.

Here's the terms we will work through:

(1) Ekklesia

(2) Metron

(3) Strongholds

(4) Gates

(5) Keys

(6) Binding/loosing

(7) Shalom

(8) Glory

Let's start with "ekklesia."

1

EKKLESIA

And Jesus answered him, "Blessed are you, Simon Bar-Jonah! For flesh and blood has not revealed this to you, but my Father who is in heaven. And I tell you, you are Peter, and on this rock I will build my church, and the gates of hell shall not prevail against it. I will give you the keys of the kingdom of heaven, and whatever you bind on earth shall be bound in heaven, and whatever you loose on earth shall be loosed in heaven." (Matthew 16:17–19)

Most Christians think they know what the church is. Most go to church regularly, though for many "regularly" means something much less regular than it did back in the day. But putting aside all unwelcome and totally unnecessary pastoral grumpiness, we should assume that most Christians think they have a grasp on what the church is.

Most would be wrong.

The church has become a weekly religious gathering where Christians gather as spectators to watch professional clergy and singers perform. Religious theater. But that's not at all what it was meant to be.

The church was originally established as the "congregation" of King Jesus, literally his kingdom assembly. In fact, the Greek word translated "church" is "ekklesia," which was a Greek word used to describe the civic assemblies of the ancient Greek world. An ekklesia in ancient times was like our city council, a legislature, a congress or a parliament. It was a place where government business was done on behalf of the community.

That's what the church was meant to be.

So the ekklesia is the kingdom assembly of King Jesus. As the Parliament of heaven, the ekklesia gathers the saints on earth with the saints in heaven (the communion of the saints), and we all are "seated together with Christ in heavenly places" conferring in the Heavenly Council with hosts of mighty angels. Christ the King ascended into heaven and now reigns over all nations. As believers, we "reign together in life" with him.

(By the way, to reign in the kingdom is to serve in love. Dominion is not domination.)

Every believer is inducted into the ekklesia when he or she is baptized into the body of Christ. Every believer is officially enrolled as Members of Parliament, as it were, and is recognized and authorized as a delegate of King Jesus and an ambassador of the kingdom.

Every believer, when he or she is baptized, signs up to become a representative of King Jesus. To become a Christian is to become a disciple, a student of King Jesus University, to pledge your fealty, loyalty and life to advance the rule of King Jesus in every nation through love.

That is quite different from sitting quietly in your seat watching others "do church" for you.

I think the biggest idea the Holy Spirit is pounding like a big bass drum is that the ekklesia is a *kingdom training center.* King Jesus assembles believers together in his ekklesia to be trained to advance his kingdom rule in the world.

At Freedom Life Church—and every church must express this in its own way—we intentionally structure every Sunday service to help believers:

- **Encounter** the Presence of God

- **Experience** heart transformation

- (be) **Equipped** in their gifts and callings

- (be) **Empowered** to serve with authority in the world

Our goal is simply to see the church restored to its original purpose of equipping people for kingdom advance during the week. In fact, we often say, "Sunday is about Monday." When believers leave, they should be prepared to enter their field, their "metron" their "area of influence."

2

METRON

But we will not boast beyond limits, but will boast only with regard to the **area of influence** God **assigned** to us, to reach even to you. For we are not overextending ourselves, as though we did not reach you. For we were the first to come all the way to you with the gospel of Christ. We do not boast beyond limit in the labors of others.

But our hope is that as your faith increases, our **area of influence** among you may be greatly enlarged, so that we may preach the gospel in lands beyond you, without boasting of work already done in another's **area of influence**. (2 Corinthians 10:13–16, emphasis added)

Every believer inducted into the ekklesia is assigned a *metron*, an "area of influence" where they are called to serve in love, to open the gates of hell, release the captives and lift up the gates so that the King of Glory may come in.

Your metron is wherever your feet walk, your hands serve, your voice speaks, your countenance shines. Your metron is wherever you have been given influence by King Jesus. Your metron is your heart, your house, your work, your world.

Your metron goes far beyond the church where you worship. In fact, the church—the ekklesia—gathers in order to equip you to serve beyond the church. Your metron is wherever you serve in every realm of life.

Every realm of life is an extension of the kingdom of God: your household, your work (which is your vocation) and your community. Jesus enlisted you when you were saved to mediate his influence and his love into every realm of life so that his glory may fill the earth.

This means that every believer must receive a true revelation of his or her assignment in every realm of life. As Paul prayed,

> That the God of our Lord Jesus Christ, the Father of glory, may give you **the Spirit of wisdom and of revelation** in the knowledge of him, having the eyes of your hearts enlightened, that you may know what is the hope to which he has called you, what are the riches of his glorious inheritance in the saints, and what is the immeasurable greatness of his power toward us who believe, according to the working of his great might that he worked in

Christ when he raised him from the dead and seated him at his right hand in the heavenly places, far above all rule and authority and power and dominion, and above every name that is named, not only in this age but also in the one to come. And he put all things under his feet and gave him as head over all things to the church, which is his body, the fullness of him who fills all in all. (Ephesians 1:17–23, emphasis added)

Then Paul declared:

But God, being rich in mercy, because of the great love with which he loved us, even when we were dead in our trespasses, made us alive together with Christ—by grace you have been saved—and raised us up with him and seated us with him in the heavenly places in Christ Jesus, so that in the coming ages he might show the immeasurable riches of his grace in kindness toward us in Christ Jesus. (Ephesians 2:4-7)

This understanding—that we are all raised with Christ, seated in heavenly places and assigned an area of influence on earth to advance the kingdom of God— requires "the spirit of wisdom and of revelation." The pull of mundane, ordinary, everyday life is intense, the persistent idea that our life is "just life," that what we live every day is materialistic, physical, visible and nothing else. We have been brainwashed by centuries of the Enlightenment to accept materialist, rationalist philosophy, and this *lie* must be broken.

The pressure to conform to mundanity is what Paul calls "the course of this world":

> And you were dead in the trespasses and sins in which you once walked, following **the course of this world**, following the prince of the power of the air, the spirit that is now at work in the sons of disobedience—among whom we all once lived in the passions of our flesh, carrying out the desires of the body and the mind, and were by nature children of wrath, like the rest of mankind. (Ephesians 2:1–7)

The course of this world is the habituated patterns of human behavior that draw people into mindless, thoughtless prejudices, biases, assumptions, mindsets, worldviews, values—just "the way things are done around here!" The kingdom of God pushes back against the course of the world and sets people on a different track, a different pathway, one that leads to life. But it takes the spirit of wisdom and revelation to escape the the soul-crushing vortex of "the spirit of the world."

Understanding that you have been called to a metron, that you have been assigned an area of influence, is the first step to breaking the mental stranglehold of the world and advancing Christ's kingdom in every nation starting in your metron.

We are baptized into the kingdom of King Jesus, and we are appointed as delegates of the ekklesia of

King Jesus, his kingdom assembly. As delegates, we represent the metrons we have been assigned. Our metron is our "district," and we represent King Jesus to our district and the people in our district to King Jesus. As Members of Parliament, we serve as kings-priests-prophets before the Lord and before the people. It is our kingdom responsibility to advance the kingdom in our metron.

3

STRONGHOLDS

For the weapons of our warfare are not of the flesh but have divine power to destroy strongholds. (2 Corinthians 10:4)

A stronghold in scripture is a metaphor (a stronghold is a fortress, a castle) used to describe human emotions, impulses, mindsets and behaviors that become patterns, habits and addictions that are exploited by Satan to dominate people.

Strongholds are *personal, familial* and *societal*. Strongholds are another way of describing "the gates of hell" that Jesus spoke about. (The "gates of hell" in Matthew 16 was also a direct reference to "the grotto of Pan," the dark powers of death.)

The gates of hell are the barriers erected by the *stoicheia.* The stoicheia are the "spirit-systems" Paul talked about in Colossians 2:8 and elsewhere that control the flow of human activity within social institutions. The stoicheia is "The System," "The Establishment" but it's more than merely human—it's filled with evil spirits. The stoicheia works to retain domination over the earth through human institutions, infiltrating society to prevent the advance of Christ's rule in the earth.

This is why evangelism often feels like hitting a wall. It does. A spirit wall. A stronghold.

- **Personal strongholds** are strongholds of the heart rooted in the emotions, the will and the mind. Personal strongholds manifest as emotional disorders, decisional and volitional impairments (addictions) and deeply ingrained mindsets (delusions) that control behavior.

- **Familial strongholds** are genetics (nature), environment (nurture) and cultural expressions carried by families. Family strongholds are family systems—the "eco-systems"—that in-grow into powerful co-dependencies that sustain the homeostasis of families. Think "clan-mentality."

- **Societal strongholds** are cultural, social pressures (the course of the world) that shape enculturated assumptions, biases, prejudices, expectations, etc. that manifest as behavior in religion, business, education, government, media and all other forms of social conformity. ("Be not conformed to this world..." — Romans 12:2)

Social strongholds usually fall into several categories. Some call these the "mountains of culture," and there are various groupings and labels for the different areas of culture by different teachers. Regardless of the variety, the basic idea is consistent and follows a similar grouping as below:

1. Family
2. Religion
3. Business
4. Government
5. Education
6. Arts & Media
7. Science & Medicine

Social strongholds are also often geographical strongholds that develop within communities, cities and nations. A regional stronghold can dominate an entire area of cities. An example of this is seen in Daniel with the "princes" of the nations and in Acts where entire cities and provinces were dominated by what Paul calls the "principalities and powers." (Ephesians 6)

Strongholds often develop at the crossroads of human activity. Strongholds of racial violence, poverty, crime, corruption, injustice, sickness, famine, drought, abuse, molestation, human trafficking, idolatry, false religion, economic exploitation, environmental exploitation, gambling addictions, on and on.

And often the actual, physical passageways of human activity—highways, intersections, crossroads, downtown areas, business centers, malls, restaurants, bars, casinos, lakefronts, beaches—become targets for demonic control and strongholds are raised through human sinful cooperation with evil powers.

Strongholds are inhabited by strongmen, evil spirits that indwell human behavior in order to gain domination over the earth. Jesus told us that we cannot "spoil the strongman's house"—which is a stronghold—until we first "bind the strongman."

> "But if it is by the Spirit of God that I cast out demons, then the kingdom of God has come upon you. Or how can someone enter a strong man's house and plunder his goods, unless he first binds the strong man? Then indeed he may plunder his house." (Matthew 12:28–29)

As The Book of Revelation puts it, strongholds are "habitations of devils." Jesus described a stronghold as a "house" (a human heart) from which demons are expelled and then return to re-inhabit seven times worse than before:

> "When the unclean spirit has gone out of a person, it passes through waterless places seeking rest, but finds none. Then it says, 'I will return to my house from which I came.' And when it comes, it finds the house empty, swept, and put in order. Then it goes and brings with it seven other spirits

more evil than itself, and they enter and dwell there, and the last state of that person is worse than the first. So also will it be with this evil generation." (Matthew 12:43–45)

Whether the strongholds are personal strongholds, familial strongholds or societal strongholds, we must know how to bind the strongman. We must first bind the strongman before we can spoil the strongman's house, which means to deliver the people taken captive by the devil "to do his will" (2 Timothy 2:26).

We bind the strongman by speaking truth. We expose lies and expel the Liar. We shall talk more about this later on when we focus on keywords. But for now, get this: strongholds are built of lies. Every lie is wrapped around a fallacy, which is the gateway— the weakest, most exposed place along the wall—to the stronghold. By speaking truth into the lie, we open a gateway that exposes the power of the strongman as a deception, a fraud and a lie.

Satan's only power is the power of a lie.

This is true of strongholds on every level. Personal, familial and societal strongholds are all broken by proclaiming the truth and commanding lying, evil spirits to go. This is what Jesus called "expelling demons." While there are certainly degrees of "demonization," every stronghold has a strongman that must be bound. We bind the strongman by using our words, which are the keys we have been given.

These keys take the form of *prayer, praise* and *prophecy.* More on that later.

Kingdom ambassadors, those inducted into the kingdom ekklesia, those serving as delegates of the King in their individual metrons, must know how to wield their keys—their *keywords*—to open the gates, bind the strongman and release the captives.

It is our kingdom responsibility to advance the kingdom in our metron, and we can only do so as we expose the strongholds, identify and bind the strongmen and open the gates for ingress/egress of the kingdom. We develop kingdom "right-of-ways" that allow renewed human, Last Adam creativity to flow through the earth for the glory of God.

4

GATES

The gates are the weakest point in any stronghold. Since strongholds are built out of lies—and this includes familial and societal strongholds—then discovering the fallacy at the heart of the lie reveals the gateway that is most vulnerable to spiritual warfare.

Gateways are openings that allow people to come and go. Just as there are *personal* strongholds, *familial* strongholds and *societal* strongholds, so there are gates in each type of stronghold.

For example, look at the gates in a *personal* stronghold.

Personal Gates

Humans were designed for the outflow and inflow of feelings, desires and ideas. Our emotions, will and mind were created porous. Not *too* porous, though— that happens when we have *no* boundaries, no fences, and relationships become toxic. Psychologists call this "enmeshment." Not cool.

Ideally, we all should have healthy boundaries, good fences. But every good fence needs a gate. Our gates are the places where we open our heart to let others in. And *out*.

Gates of the heart were created for the free flow of emotions, desires and thoughts. My emotions flow out and influence you; your emotions flow back and influence me. Same with impulses and ideas. This is the basis for all relationships. Give and take.

Healthy people are open to emotion, desires and ideas, but they also know when to shut the gate and refuse entry to intrusive people. Mature management of the "gates" is one of the best measures of mental health.

Simple self-control.

But when humans fell into sin, the evil one gained access to the gateways of the human heart. Now, the unregenerate emotions, will and mind are highly susceptible to lies. Through delusions, Satan seizes control of the ingress/egress of the human heart.

When a strongman gains control of the gates of our heart, he can manipulate our emotions, impulses and ideas. He can also sabotage healthy relationships and shut out people who love us deeply. He uses lies to entangle us with destructive people while closing us off from those who influence us for good.

If you've ever seen someone under the domination of a spiritual stronghold, you know exactly what I'm talking about. It's not pretty.

And we've all been there on some level at some time or another.

(Another form of "gates" that we often hear about are the "head-gates," the eye-gate; the ear-gate; the mouth-gate—even the nose-gate, recognizing the often underestimated power of smell to evoke emotion, desires and thoughts.)

When the strongman establishes a stronghold within the human heart, the only way deliverance comes is for someone who knows the truth of the gospel to declare the truth into the heart and penetrate the web of lies Satan has spun.

As Paul puts it,

> For the weapons of our warfare are not of the flesh but have divine power to destroy strongholds. We destroy arguments and every lofty opinion raised against the knowledge of God, and take every thought captive to obey Christ. (2 Corinthians 10:4–5)

Familial & Societal Strongholds

The same is true of *familial* and *societal* strongholds: the truth of the gospel exposes the lie that buttresses the fortress and exposes the fallacy that opens the way into the stronghold so that the strongman may be bound by the truth of Christ's victory over the Powers at the cross.

People who believe the gospel—believers!—are called to scout out the strongholds in families, neighborhoods, cities, regions and nations and discover the gateways that expose the strongman.

For example, the stronghold of poverty is built on the lie that money—or better, Mammon—is god. In gold we trust. (And, ironically, the spirit of poverty controls both the rich and the poor, anyone who "trusts in uncertain riches.") The truth of the gospel exposes the lie and delivers the captives.

Sometimes strongholds develop in actual, physical gateways of human activity—highways, intersections, downtown areas, schools, universities, business centers, office complexes, sports arenas, malls, restaurants, bars, clubs, casinos, lakefronts, beaches— and evil spirits cluster at the crossroads of human activity.

When this happens, a spiritual gateway can be perceived by those who discern spiritual currents and demonic activity in a city or region. By physically praying, prophesying and praising the one true God at the site of the gateway, believers can shift the balance of power in an area and release the kingdom of God.

Corrupted gateways become portals for evil spirits and shrines to false gods. Idol worship always follows demonic activity. Then the places where idols are worshipped become "high places," and demons gather there to enforce and exploit the delusion.

The idols may be overt (as in explicit false gods) or they may be covert (gods such as money, sex and power). The hidden idols of the Western world are more insidious than the obvious idols of so-called primitive people. Idols enthroned on money, sex and power are often disguised as "just life." This makes them all the more challenging to expose and expel.

Believers must identify the "high places" of a region and confront the lie with the truth: the proclamation of the gospel through prayer, praise and prophecy. And this must be done in close physical proximity. Believers must take dominion over the gates of hell.

This locating of spiritual strongholds and gateways is called *spiritual mapping.*

As I worked through these notes and prepared to teach, I kept catching a glimpse in my mind of a "warren" of streets and alleyways like an ancient city with gateways blocking entrance to various parts of the city. I kept hearing that everyone's metron intersects with the stoicheia used by the Powers to dominate human activity. And it is the calling of every believer to discover the strongholds and gateways in their metron so that the gates can be opened for the King of Glory to come in.

I kept hearing that every believer must be trained in spiritual mapping. Otherwise, they will be kicked around, tossed to and fro, by demonic powers they don't even know they're up against. They will face a stronghold within their metron at work and write it all off as "just inter-office politics," just "workplace drama." But if they become sensitive to the spiritual reality of the world around us, they will discern a stronghold and discover gateways where truth can be declared in love and the demonic lie is broken.

I know just a little about spiritual mapping. When we came to Mansfield in 2017 to plant Freedom Life Church, the Holy Spirit spoke to me in the middle of the night and told me, "You are up against an old spirit of injustice." At that time, we had no idea about the violent history of Mansfield, the racial conflict surrounding the integration of Mansfield schools in 1956 and ongoing struggles for equity and justice. I've spent the last few years learning everything I can about the history of our beautiful but conflicted city.

The Father also revealed that we are breaking through to the strongman of this city, which is "Mammon." And now, Holy Spirit is giving us strategies for advancing further into the next season and era of the kingdom in Mansfield.

God has great things in mind for Mansfield!

I think every believer needs to hear about spiritual mapping, to learn from the military-style scouting—

reconnoitering—done by the 10 spies and later by Joshua as they took Jericho and entered the land. We need to identify the strongholds and strongmen in the metron we have been assigned.

If we do not identity the spirits we are up against, we will fight blindly. We will be up against inter-office politics and not know that it is demonic. We will face sexual harassment, racism, and other forms of oppression that Satan uses to dominate humans. He provokes fear and sets people against each other in order to control them. Spiritual mapping allows us to identify in prayer what we're dealing with.

We need to learn how to do spiritual mapping in our homes, our jobs, our neighborhoods and our community. We *must* develop the skills to see in the spirit and know what we're dealing with.

Possessing the Gates of the Enemy

God's strategy for saving the world is to send believers out as kingdom ambassadors, kingdom operatives, who advance the rule of Jesus by enacting Christ's dominion over the gates of the enemy within our metron. As God said to Abraham, our father in faith, we are called to possess the gates of our enemies.

> And the angel of the Lord called to Abraham a second time from heaven and said, "By myself I have sworn, declares the Lord, because you have done this and have not withheld your son, your

only son, I will surely bless you, and I will surely multiply your offspring as the stars of heaven and as the sand that is on the seashore.

And your offspring shall possess the gate of his enemies, and in your offspring shall all the nations of the earth be blessed, because you have obeyed my voice." (Genesis 22:15–18)

God's plan is that we should receive keys that open the gates that hell has dominated and that the gates should be possessed by the promised seed. To possess the gates is to gain authority and dominion in your metron insomuch that through your influence the King of glory can come in.

Lift up your heads, O gates! And be lifted up, O ancient doors, that the King of glory may come in. Who is this King of glory? The Lord, strong and mighty, the Lord, mighty in battle! Lift up your heads, O gates! And lift them up, O ancient doors, that the King of glory may come in. Who is this King of glory? The Lord of hosts, he is the King of glory! Selah (Psalm 24:7-10)

Every believer has been assigned a metron so that they may identify and unlock the gates of their metron so that the King of glory may come in. The goal is glory. The *fullness* of glory. That the earth may be filled with "the knowledge of the glory of the Lord as the waters cover the sea" (Habakuk 2:14).

The Gates of Heaven

One final thing. Our focus here is the gates of hell. But there are also "gates of heaven."

> Then Jacob awoke from his sleep and said, "Surely the Lord is in this place, and I did not know it." And he was afraid and said, "How awesome is this place! This is none other than the house of God, and this is the gate of heaven." (Genesis 28:16–17)

Just as we open the gates of hell in our metron, so we open the gates of heaven. We release the atmosphere of heaven everywhere we go.

When we praise, pray and prophesy, we open the gates of heaven, Bethel, where the glory of the Lord breaks through and the angels ascend and descend. As we gain authority in our metron, we discover just like Jacob did old altars where the ground has been consecrated to the Lord, places where intercessors from previous generations cried out for healing in the land.

And then we partner in covenant with God at these "Bethel gateways" so that the blessing of Abraham may flow into the earth. And when believers find openings, Bethel gateways, we must release covenant blessing into our metron.

But that's another book.

5

KEYS

Here we are—finally at the destination we've been winding our way toward from the start: *keywords*. First, though, let's glance back at where we've been.

Believers are inducted into the kingdom ekklesia of King Jesus and assigned a metron, a district where they represent God to people and people to God.

Every metron within the world is filled with personal, familial and societal strongholds tyrannized by strongmen, evil powers who consolidate control over people through lies.

In every stronghold, which is built of lies, there are gateways, fallacies that are vulnerable to truth. (Sometimes the gateways are physical locations.)

Believers are called to discover where the strongholds are within their metron and what lies buttress the delusion. Once the lie is exposed, the strongman can be identified and bound. When the strongman is bound, the captives can be liberated.

This means, for example, that believers must approach their vocation—their *job*—as a "Land of Promise" that they are called to walk through like Abraham and release covenant blessing.

When we arrive on Day One at a new job, we should walk on the premises having spent time in prayer seeking the wisdom of God for how to serve humbly in love—and *also how to discern the spiritual climate* of our workplace. Only through the Holy Spirit can we perceive the "warrens" of political and social interaction, the relational and interactional clusters, that are exploited by Satan to dominate people.

Stop now and think: how much have you experienced workplace settings sabotaged by inter-office politics and social drama that paralyzes the creative and service purpose of your company? How much have you seen evil powers manipulate competition and rivalry in a dehumanizing way? We have all seen it. But we must *see what we see.* We must recognize the strongholds rising ominously before us.

As Jesus said, he will build his ekklesia and the gates of hell will not prevail against it. When you are sent out by the ekklesia of King Jesus, you represent his rule on your job. You are an ambassador. You are a kingdom operative. Your assignment is to bind the strongman, throw wide the gates, deliver entranced people and usher in the King of Glory.

By the way, this is not the forceful, violent imposition of Christianity—it is the release of the love of Christ into a workplace that doesn't have to be explicitly Christian to function according to kingdom principles. Of course, we want everyone to encounter the Presence of Jesus and be saved, but the blessing of Abraham positively impacts everyone it touches, even those who are not yet followers of Jesus. *This is what it means to be salt and light!*

"You are the salt of the earth, but if salt has lost its taste, how shall its saltiness be restored? It is no longer good for anything except to be thrown out and trampled under people's feet."

"You are the light of the world. A city set on a hill cannot be hidden. Nor do people light a lamp and put it under a basket, but on a stand, and it gives light to all in the house. In the same way, let your light shine before others, so that they may see your good works and give glory to your Father who is in heaven." (Matthew 5:13–16)

After declaring that the gates of hell will not prevail against the ekklesia, Jesus promised to give believers the keys of the kingdom of heaven. This means that Jesus authorizes believers within the ekklesia and sends us out empowered to bind the strongmen of every stronghold.

The keys represent authority. The keys represent access. Believers are sent out as *key-people.*

Words Are Keys

So what are the keys? As the Holy Spirit said to me, "Words are keys." The keys are declarations. The keys of the kingdom of heaven are the words that we declare in the face of every stronghold. We speak to the gates and command them to open. We pray, praise and prophesy over the gates. We declare the truth in the face of every lie.

Every Christian must learn the importance of the words we speak. (Words create your world.)

The keys that open the gates to every stronghold are the words that we declare over them. But the words that we speak must be more than mere language—our words are not mantras, spells, magical formulas. The words that we speak must align with the words of God, and they must carry the weight of experience.

Only words mixed with faith—and faith entails faithfulness, i.e., experience and testimony—carry the weight of God's word. And when we speak the words of God that we have lived and proved through times of testing, then those words mixed with faith become keys that open the gates. This is "the word of their *testimony.*"

And I heard a loud voice in heaven, saying, "Now the salvation and the power and the kingdom of our God and the authority of his Christ have come, for the accuser of our brothers has been thrown down, who accuses them day and night before our God. And they have conquered him by the blood of the Lamb and by the **word** of their **testimony**, for they loved not their lives even unto death. (Revelation 12:10–11, emphasis added):

Words gain weight. When the words we have received—both the direct promises of Scripture and the prophetic words spoken from our destiny—are tested, the words grow in authority and presence. Just like Joseph:

> Until what [Joseph] had said came to pass, the word of the Lord tested him. (Psalm 105:19)

Joseph was tested to increase his capacity for glory, his capacity for kingdom responsibility. We are never tested to make us fail—we are always tested to certify us for greater glory. When we "decree a thing" but have never endured a test related to that word, the word carries little weight. But when the word we've spoken has tested us like Joseph, then we are brought into places of authority where our word carries weight.

"The words of the Lord are pure, like silver in a furnace of earth purified seven times" (Psalm 12:6). The fire of testing purifies fleshly agendas that threaten glory and undermine blessing. God's glory would crush us without the testing. What would have happened to Joseph if he'd received the keys to Egypt as a teenager?

It would be like giving my car keys to our seven-year-old twins. *Right.*

We gain "ranks" (like Paul said of deacons in 1 Timothy 3:13) of authority in the heavens as we pass tests and are certified for kingdom rule that manifests in the earth. (Think of David.) Then, as we gain rank and certification, our words carry authority in the earth (favor with God and man) and open gateways into new realms of kingdom influence and our metron is enlarged. (Jabez)

Keycards

The keywords we are given are like keycards that give us access to different levels of authority. We gain authority through testimony. We are certified by testing. And each layer of authority that we receive is gained by experience, and this gives weight to our words, which means that our keywords—our keycard —will open doors for us that others could not open.

Two powerful stories that illustrate this idea come to mind.

First story: remember when the disciples tried to cast the demons out of the little boy and could not? They were furiously swiping their keycards, but no good. Then Jesus walks down from the mountain and —one swipe!—the demons flees in terror.

They asked Jesus why. He replied, "Faith. Simple faith. Faith that has grown through prayer and fasting." The disciples simply didn't have access on their keycard due to untrained faith.

Faith grows as the "word of faith," the "prayer of faith" and the "test of faith" grows.

> Count it all joy, my brothers, when you meet trials of various kinds, for you know that the testing of your faith produces steadfastness. And let steadfastness have its full effect, that you may be perfect and complete, lacking in nothing. (James 1:2–4)

The second story is one of my favorite childhood Sunday School stories. I loved it! Probably for all the wrong reasons. It is the story of the seven sons of Sceva:

> Then some of the itinerant Jewish exorcists undertook to invoke the name of the Lord Jesus over those who had evil spirits, saying, "I adjure you by the Jesus whom Paul proclaims." Seven sons of a Jewish high priest named Sceva were doing this. But the evil spirit answered them, "Jesus I know, and Paul I recognize, but who are you?"

> And the man in whom was the evil spirit leaped on them, mastered all of them and overpowered them, so that they fled out of that house naked and wounded. And this became known to all the residents of Ephesus, both Jews and Greeks. And

fear fell upon them all, and the name of the Lord Jesus was extolled. (Acts 19:13–17)

As a kid, when I would imagine seven naked white tails disappearing down the road, I would laugh until the tears flowed. Too good.

Of course, the point here is a bit more reverent than my childhood memories. The seven sons of Sceva simply didn't have the authority to expel that demon. They had found Paul's keycard—the declaration of the name "Jesus"—but they had no faith (faithfulness, experience, testimony) with it.

Words are not enough. We must use words that gain weight, words that have been tested and proved. Words that carry the weight of glory, certifications that demonstrate God's trust in *us*, not just our trust in him.

God's trust in *us* is called *favor.*

Each experience that we have with God deepens the weight of our words, and when we speak we gain authority over what we have experienced. We name it and tame it. This increases our access through the gates of hell in our assigned metron.

Jesus talked about "the key of David":

"And to the angel of the church in Philadelphia write: 'The words of the holy one, the true one, who has the key of David, who opens and no one will shut, who shuts and no one opens. I know your works. Behold, I have set before you an open door, which no one is able to shut. I know that you have but little power, and yet you have kept my word and have not denied my name.'" (Revelation 3:7–8)

The Key of David opens and shuts the treasury and the armory of David. This is the ultimate keycard!

Our prayer must be, "Father, help me find my keys!" Every metron has strongholds with gates that can only be opened with the keys of the kingdom of heaven—which is nothing less than, "What is the Holy Spirit saying *right now* into this gate?"

Every gate in our metron can only be opened through the truth of the gospel declared over and over with the weight of testimony. As we confront the gates of hell in our metron, we must hear what Holy Spirit is saying and sing it, say it, shout it until the truth breaks the lie.

What are you saying? When the word God gives you is tested, will you remain faithful to say *only* what the Father is saying? This is the key: refuse to say anything other than what the Father is saying. Refuse to empower the strongman by agreeing with his lies, by speaking the words of the enemy. No, we must speak only what God is saying!

The truth will break the power of the lie.

6

BINDING & LOOSING

W e gain authority through testimony. Our faith is tested, and experience qualifies us for greater glory.

Here's James again—it's worth repeating:

Count it all joy, my brothers, when you meet trials of various kinds, for you know that the testing of your faith produces steadfastness. And let steadfastness have its full effect, that you may be perfect and complete, lacking in nothing. (James 1:2–4)

This is not about degrees of God's love for us—he loves all of us infinitely. But it is about favor. Favor grows through obedience and experience:

And he said to them, "Why were you looking for me? Did you not know that I must be in my Father's house?" And they did not understand the saying that he spoke to them. And he went down with them and came to Nazareth and was submissive to them. And his mother treasured up all these things in her heart. And Jesus increased in wisdom and in stature and in favor with God and man. (Luke 2:49–52)

As Hebrews says:

Although [Jesus] was a son, he learned obedience through what he suffered. (Hebrews 5:8)

Jesus was tested as a young boy in the temple, in the wilderness after his baptism and when he agonized in Gethsemane. But he demonstrated his perfect obedience and his infallible qualification to be King of Glory through the cross.

We also must be tested. Words have power, and the Father must be sure that he can trust us with the keys to the kingdom of heaven. And no wonder, for the keys to the kingdom of heaven carry tremendous power to shift human history and release the mighty power of God. As Jesus said,

"I will give you the keys of the kingdom of heaven, and whatever you bind on earth shall be bound in heaven, and whatever you loose on earth shall be loosed in heaven." (Matthew 16:19)

"Binding and loosing" in Scripture refers back to the Jewish idea that the Rabbis had the authority to permit and forbid behavior. The Jews believed that the Sanhedrin was a "lower house of judgment to which the upper, heavenly house of judgment gave its supreme sanction." Jesus' statement on "binding and loosing" follows perfectly from Jesus' usage of the "ekklesia"—the church on earth rules in alignment with the heavenly sanctuary, the throne room of King Jesus.

This is why we must see the church as the ekklesia. We must understand the empowering, authorizing role that the gathered church exercises. You as a believer are empowered to execute the edicts of King Jesus in the earth.

In fact, the phrase "whatever you bind on earth will be bound in heaven" is better rendered "whatever you bind on earth *having been bound* in heaven." This shows the interactive nature of the ekklesia: we gather to be *equipped* and *empowered* as delegates of King Jesus.

We then go out into the world and enact what he has instructed us to do: heal the sick, raise the dead, expel demons, preach the gospel, be salt and light, feed the hungry, clothe the naked, bind up the broken-hearted, liberate the captives, declare the year of jubilee. *This is what we are called to do Monday through Friday!*

Sunday is about Monday.

The church has little right to complain about the state of the world when the church rarely exercises its own authority in the world. The gates of hell cannot prevail as long as the church is binding and loosing what King Jesus decrees. But the church has been privatized. We have been sequestered, cloistered and quarantined—and that was long before COVID-19!

The church bought the lie a long time ago that "the separation of church and state" demands that we remain hidden within the private, pietistic realm of religion. But the kingdom of God cannot be contained. The ekklesia of Jesus is on the rise! We are recovering the revelation that brings a revolution: the revelation of our authority in the world.

Again, this is not about imposing Christianity Crusade-style. But it is about getting out of our four walls and releasing the rule of Jesus into our metron. We are called to bind and loose, to decree the words of Jesus over every gateway in our metron until every strongman is bound and every captive is loosed.

Think about your metron: are you consciously, intentionally approaching your job—your vocation— as your authorized, empowered kingdom responsibility? Do you bind and loose at work? Do you wield the keys of authority and open the gates of creational stewardship so that the King of Glory may come in? Are you interceding for your co-workers? Are you declaring the promises of God and the blessing of Abraham where you live, work and play?

If not, it's time to start right now.

This is a significant shift in our thinking. We too often think our authority comes from the earth, from our boss or our company. But Paul makes it clear that Christian employees receive their dominion mandate—their authority to rule through serving on earth—from King Jesus.

Who hired you? Jesus did. And your employer is contracting with you and King Jesus for your temporary services. You "serve the Lord Christ."

Employees, obey in everything those who are your earthly bosses, not by way of eye-service, as people-pleasers, but with sincerity of heart, fearing the Lord. Whatever you do, work heartily, as for the Lord and not for men, knowing that from the Lord you will receive the inheritance as your reward. You are serving the Lord Christ. (Colossians 3:22–24)

It's time to bind and loose on earth as it is in heaven. And here's what I mean by that:

(1) Attend ekklesia gatherings where you are equipped and empowered.

(2) Go home and bind the lies of Satan over your heart and over your family. Loose the promises of God over your heart and over your family. Bind every strongman that has taken up evil residence in the strongholds of your heart and your family. Use your words! Your words are keys. As you continue to declare the promises of God even in the face of delay and disappointment, your words gain weight. Keep praying, praising and prophesying the promises of God.

(3) Then, turn your focus toward your external metron. Start declaring the promises of God over your work and world. Ask God for discernment to discover the strongholds that dominate your workplace. Ask Holy Spirit to unmask the strongman that manipulates and dominates the people who move in and out of the gateways in your workplace. Become intentional about intercession over your metron. Ask Abba Father for wisdom to bring truth into the lies that control the narrative, the business strategies, the workplace culture that shape the ethos of your workplace. Bind and loose with the words you speak. Use the keys you have been given to bring long term, positive change in your workplace.

You have authority. Your authority grows as you persevere in prayer, praise and prophecy. Like the widow who wouldn't stop asking the judge for justice (Luke 18), the prayer of faith is the prayer that won't stop praying. Your keys are "cut" and "grooved" through perseverance. Keep praying!

7

SHALOM

We are called to release shalom into our metron. Shalom is most often translated "peace," and that's certainly true; but there is much more to shalom than peace, more than "absence of conflict." Shalom means "wholeness" and "well-being." Many Bible versions translate shalom as "welfare."

So, when we say that we are called to mediate shalom into our metron, we mean that we are called to mediate wholeness: the un-fragmented human existence and stewardship over creation that God originally envisioned when he created all things.

God made creation whole; sin divided it. Sin fragmented and disintegrated human existence through the curse that brought corruption to all creation. This fragmentation is what Scripture calls "brokenhearted-ness." Shalom restores union between God and people, and re-unites human identity with the image of God.

The defragmentation of the human heart—the restoration of the integrated self—is what we call "inner healing," when the shalom of God makes the heart whole. The human spirit is realigned with God's Spirit; the soul is reintegrated emotionally, volitionally and intellectually; and the body manifests the healed self. The neural pathways of the brain that have developed around trauma and dissociated consciousness and sub-consciousness, impulse and awareness, are realigned with God, self and others, and the person becomes whole.

This wholeness—this shalom—is meant to manifest externally through relationships into family and society. Just as "hurt people hurt people," "healed people heal people." This is God's strategy for releasing healing into the earth.

Creation groans for healing, as Paul put it:

> For the creation waits with eager longing for the revealing of the sons of God. For the creation was subjected to futility, not willingly, but because of him who subjected it, in hope that the creation itself will be set free from its bondage to corruption and obtain the freedom of the glory of the children of God. For we know that the whole creation has been groaning together in the pains of childbirth until now. (Romans 8:19–22)

Creation longs for the revelation of the sons of God, the manifestation of the children of God. The sons and daughters of God "manifest" by stepping into their kingdom authority and mediating the rule of Jesus into the world. Creation is groaning for this. Creation cries for shalom.

The idea of releasing shalom into the world is most explicitly set out in Jeremiah 29:

> Thus says the Lord of hosts, the God of Israel, to all the exiles whom I have sent into exile from Jerusalem to Babylon:
>
> "Build houses and live in them; plant gardens and eat their produce. Take wives and have sons and daughters; take wives for your sons, and give your daughters in marriage, that they may bear sons and daughters; multiply there, and do not decrease. But seek the welfare [shalom] of the city where I have sent you into exile, and pray to the Lord on its behalf, for in its welfare [shalom] you will find your welfare [shalom]." (Jeremiah 29:4-7)

Look at how everyday the instruction was: build houses, plant gardens, have children. And while living everyday life, pray for the city. Pray for the shalom of the city. Pray for the wholeness of the city.

What does shalom look like? Sociologists measure shalom as "well-being" or "human flourishing."

Here's an example:

State of American Well-Being

The "State of American Well-Being" report, part of the Gallup-Sharecare State of American Well-Being series, examines well-being across the nation, with 186 communities ranked based on their Well-Being Index scores. The report analyzes how well-being varies by community and across the five elements of well-being:

- **Purpose**: liking what you do each day and being motivated to achieve your goal.

- **Social**: having supportive relationships and love in your life

- **Financial**: managing your economic life to reduce stress and increase security

- **Community**: liking where you live, feeling safe, and having pride in your community

- **Physical**: having good health and enough energy to get things done daily

Here's another study, this one done on "human flourishing." The "Human Flourishing Program at Harvard's Institute for Quantitative Social Science" lists six "domains of human flourishing":

- Domain 1: Happiness and Life Satisfaction

- Domain 2: Mental and Physical Health

- Domain 3: Meaning and Purpose

- Domain 4: Character and Virtue

- Domain 5: Close Social Relationships

- Domain 6: Financial and Material Stability

But a seventh—or, rather, the *first!*—domain is missing: relationship with Creator God. The only way human flourishing can be sustained is through a restoration of relationship between humans and the God who formed them. Because humans were made in the image of God, shalom only comes in fullness through the kingdom of God.

Look back to Jeremiah 29 and notice the interplay of shalom:

"For in the shalom of the city you will find your shalom."

Note the cycle, the circle, of shalom: Believers intercede for the shalom of the city and the city receives shalom. Then, the shalom of the city circles back and becomes "your shalom." There is a mutuality of shalom, a shalom-synergy, that develops.

This cycle-of-shalom becomes what the Bible calls the "fullness" (Greek: *"pleroma"*) of glory that fills the earth as the waters cover the sea. When the kingdom of God releases shalom into the nations through the metrons of believers, then the blessing of Abraham upon the nations returns back upon the people of God as the full harvest of glory.

Those who follow Jesus actually share in the glory of God and enjoy the fullness of joy that comes in his

Presence. The shalom that we have released comes back like bread upon the water, like seed sown in tears and reaped in joy. Just like the natural harvest, we always reap more than we sow.

We find our fullness in accepting our responsibility to steward shalom in our metron. As our family, our workplace, our church, our neighborhood, our world prospers, we prosper.

As the shalom of the kingdom becomes the shalom of the city and the shalom of the city becomes the shalom of the kingdom, the purpose of God is worked out in the world. Jeremiah continues:

> For thus says the Lord: "When seventy years are completed for Babylon, I will visit you, and I will fulfill to you my promise and bring you back to this place. For I know the plans I have for you, declares the Lord, plans for welfare [shalom] and not for evil, to give you a future and a hope."
>
> "Then you will call upon me and come and pray to me, and I will hear you. You will seek me and find me, when you seek me with all your heart. I will be found by you, declares the Lord, and I will restore your fortunes and gather you from all the nations and all the places where I have driven you, declares the Lord, and I will bring you back to the place from which I sent you into exile." (Jeremiah 29:10)

The purpose of God in the world, the coming of his kingdom among all nations, is directly tied up with the incarnational and intercessional ministry of the ekklesia.

And here's the kicker: your personal destiny is directly tied to the fulfilling of God's big-picture purpose in the earth. As Jesus said, "Seek first the kingdom of heaven and its righteousness and all these things—the things *you* need!—will be added to you." When you seek the shalom of the city your personal shalom, your human flourishing, will blossom.

We all have a deep, personal interest in pursuing the shalom of the city. It's how we fulfill our purpose, our vocation, our call. Do you want to find personal fulfillment? Then get caught up in the kingdom agenda of King Jesus!

Bottom line? We must receive a revelation of our assignment: to mediate shalom in our metron, to bring healing, defragmentation, reintegration into a terminally divided culture. We are reconcilers! We received the "ministry of reconciliation." We are wholeness-exporters. The divisions that have broken down the human race are erased in Christ, and the ekklesia models what creational unity looks like (unity-in-diversity) and mediates that unity to the world—and we do this as we do so within our metron.

We are responsible for our metron to see atmospheres shift, gates open, strongholds falls, strongmen bound and people delivered from the curse of sin and death. We must take personally the well-being of our home, neighborhood, workplace, community, nation and world. We are not observers, critics and complainers. We are not armchair quarterbacks. We are not back-seat drivers. We are not spectators in the stands heaping abuse on the team below. We *are* the team! We are on the field.

We must get in the game.

8

GLORY

For the earth will be filled with the knowledge of the glory of the Lord as the waters cover the sea. (Habakkuk 2:14)

The ultimate goal of creation is glory.

The glory of the Lord is the manifestation of the qualities of God. Glory is the full effect—though there are degrees of glory. The beauty of the Lord, the wisdom of the Lord, the power of the Lord, the love of the Lord, the grandeur of the Lord, the majesty of the Lord, the wealth of the Lord, the faithfulness of the Lord, the holiness of the Lord—any of the attributes of the Lord manifest is glory. And as the manifestation of the Lord's attributes increases, glory increases.

The Greek word for "glory" in the New Testament is "*doxa*." Doxa corresponds to the Old Testament word "*kabod*," which carries the idea of "heaviness, or weightiness" as it relates metaphorically to "worthiness." The glory of the Lord is called "the eternal weight of glory" (2 Corinthians 4:17).

The goal is glory. The reason Abba Father sent us into the world is to release his glory into the earth. We carry glory:

> But when one turns to the Lord, the veil is removed. Now the Lord is the Spirit, and where the Spirit of the Lord is, there is freedom. And we all, with unveiled face, beholding the glory of the Lord, are being transformed into the same image from one degree of glory to another. For this comes from the Lord who is the Spirit. (2 Corinthians 3:16–18)

God will not give his glory to another, but he does share his glory. He created us to be glorified. Glory is our destiny. And we mediate glory into the world by manifesting the Presence of God in our metron.

And I don't just mean charismatic manifestations of the Spirit such as the gifts of the Spirit, though they certainly may work in the world as we serve through love. But I mean manifestations more in terms of the blessing of Abraham taking root in human behavior. I mean the actual transformation of human society through kingdom influence.

Kingdom influence is mediated to the world as wisdom, power and love. When we offer wisdom as solutions to intractable problems; when we demonstrate the mighty power of God through miracles, healings, signs and wonders, through the power of a transformed life; when we serve in love; we mediate kingdom influence into the world.

The blessing of Abraham, the shalom that we spoke about earlier, releases the glory of God into the world. When we use our keywords to fling open the gates, expose the strongholds and expel the strongman, then transformation comes and the glory of the Lord rises in our metron. I am talking about the increase of all the qualities of human flourishing. Life gets better when the glory of the Lord is released.

Creation groans for glory. As Paul said,

I am convinced that any suffering we endure is less than nothing compared to the magnitude of glory that is about to be unveiled within us. The entire universe is standing on tiptoe, yearning to see the unveiling of God's glorious sons and daughters! For against its will the universe itself has had to endure the empty futility resulting from the consequences of human sin. But now, with eager expectation, all creation longs for freedom from its slavery to decay and to experience with us the wonderful freedom coming to God's children.

To this day we are aware of the universal agony and groaning of creation, as if it were in the contractions of labor for childbirth. And it's not just creation. We who have already experienced the first fruits of the Spirit also inwardly groan as we passionately long to experience our full status as God's sons and daughters—including our physical bodies being transformed. For this is the hope of our salvation. (Romans 8:18–24, TPT)

Glory is manifest. Glory is very practical. Glory impacts and transforms everyday, real-world life. When humans behold the glory of the Lord they are transformed into the same image from glory to glory —"from one degree of glory to another." As kingdom ambassadors manifest glory in their metrons all over the world, and their metrons begin to manifest shalom, the earth begins to be filled with the glory of the Lord.

And get this: filling the earth with glory is not a sudden, all-at-once global event that erupts spontaneously all over the earth. No, Jesus made it clear that the glory of God would fill the earth like a small mustard see grows into a large tree; like yeast that leavens dough—slowly, surely, finally and fully.

He said therefore, "What is the kingdom of God like? And to what shall I compare it? It is like a grain of mustard seed that a man took and sowed in his garden, and it grew and became a tree, and the birds of the air made nests in its branches."

And again he said, "To what shall I compare the kingdom of God? It is like leaven that a woman took and hid in three measures of flour, until it was all leavened." (Luke 13:18–21)

The glory of the Lord fills the earth as millions upon millions of believers bring transformation into their metron.

Paul calls this gradual transformation "fullness" (pleroma). The idea of fullness pervades Paul's writing, and it flows from our opening verse:

> For the earth will be filled with the knowledge of the glory of the Lord as the waters cover the sea. (Habakkuk 2:14)

The fullness of glory—which is the full display of God's attributes manifest in the earth—is the goal of everything we do. As Revelation puts it,

> Then I looked, and I heard around the throne and the living creatures and the elders the voice of many angels, numbering myriads of myriads and thousands of thousands, saying with a loud voice, "Worthy is the Lamb who was slain, to receive power and wealth and wisdom and might and honor and glory and blessing!"
>
> And I heard every creature in heaven and on earth and under the earth and in the sea, and all that is in them, saying, "To him who sits on the throne and to the Lamb be blessing and honor and glory and might forever and ever!" And the four living creatures said, "Amen!" and the elders fell down and worshiped. (Revelation 5:11–14)

This level of praise is our goal, to see Jesus glorified in the earth.

As we saw earlier, the reason we open the gates of hell is to allow the King of Glory to enter into our metron and restore creation back to its original purpose. As the we use our keys, open the gates, bind the strongman, subdue the strongholds and release the captives, creation emerges from the chaos of the curse and rediscovers its original purpose.

Humans are re-humanized. Families are re-united in healthy relations. Society returns to the living God. All the markers of human suffering begin to decline in the light of God's glory and grace. The deceiver of the nations is bound, and the King of Glory rides in to the praise of the nations!

SUMMARY & CONCLUSION

Let's look back over what we've covered:

(1) Ekklesia

(2) Metron

(3) Strongholds

(4) Gates

(5) Keys

(6) Binding/loosing

(7) Shalom

(8) Glory

So, what do we do?

(1) Find a church that will be a kingdom ekklesia, a church that will equip you to be a kingdom operative. The days of spectator church are over.

(2) Take the ekklesia home and make your house a kingdom household. The church was never meant to gather only in public assemblies. It was *always* meant to gather both "in the temple and from house-to-house."

(3) Survey the boundaries of your metron—make sure you know where you are called to serve. Once you have marked out the boundaries of your metron, become intentional about praying, praising and prophesying over it. Baptize your "area of influence" with intercession. Start spiritual mapping to discover where the strongholds are and who the strongmen are. Then, use the keys Holy Spirit has cut in your voice—your keywords!—and start declaring the truth of the gospel into the lies that buttress the fortress of evil in your metron.

(4) Serve in love in your metron and seek first the kingdom in all you do. Persevere in prayer until victory manifests. Don't let discouragement win! Pray, praise and prophesy until the gates open, the strongman is bound and the stronghold falls. Keep persevering until shalom permeates every square inch of your metron, until the blessing of Abraham transforms your sphere and the King of Glory rides through your gates.

(5) And all of this begins with a revelation—a revelation of what we are called to do. Ask the Father to open your eyes that you may see what he is doing in the world.

Now, go change the world!

Made in the USA
Columbia, SC
14 January 2022

54042182R00040